SCiENCE
Workbook

Level 1

MOONSTONE

Published in Moonstone
by Rupa Publications India Pvt. Ltd 2022
7/16, Ansari Road, Daryaganj
New Delhi 110002

Sales centres:
Allahabad Bengaluru Chennai
Hyderabad Jaipur Kathmandu
Kolkata Mumbai

ISBN: 978-93-5520-706-7

First impression 2022

10 9 8 7 6 5 4 3 2 1

The moral right of the authors has been asserted.

Printed in India

Contents

Our Surroundings

The area around us is called our surroundings. We should keep our surroundings clean and green.

A. Look at the picture given below. Identify and name the objects you can see. Can you try to find them in your surroundings too?

B. Can you tick (✔) the things which you can find in your surroundings?

C. Circle the things which make our surroundings dirty.

D. Name three things which you see around your house.

E. Name three things which you see around your school.

F. Fill in the blanks with the help of the box given below.

trees	Dirty	clean	Plants	dustbin

1. We should keep our surroundings _____.

2. _____ surroundings can make us fall ill.

3. We should throw the waste into the _____.

4. _____ keep the air fresh and clean.

5. We should plant more _____.

5

Living and Non-living Things

All the things around us are either living or non-living.

Living things can breathe, move, grow and reproduce. They need food to stay alive. All animals and plants are living things.

Non-living things do not move, breathe, grow or reproduce. Objects such as table, pencil, paper and toy are non-living things.

A. Look at the images given below and write **L** for living things and **N** for non-living things.

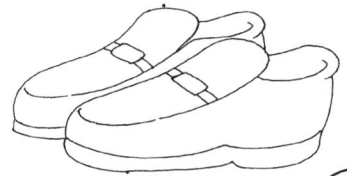

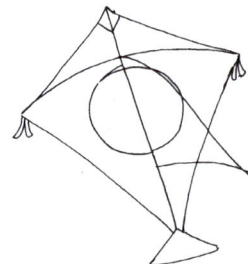

B. **Name three living things.**

C. **Name three non-living things.**

D. **Name three non-living things which you need to stay alive.**

E. **Fill in the blanks with the correct answer in each of the following questions.**

1. Animals and plants need air to _____.

move		breathe

2. Living things need _____ to live.

water		gold

3. _____ things cannot reproduce.

Living		Non-living

4. Plants need _____ to grow.

animals		soil

5. Living things need _____ to eat.

food		air

Natural and Man-made Things

The things which we get from nature are called natural things. People use natural things to make objects they need. These are called man-made things.

All living things are natural and all man-made things are non-living.

A. Look at the pictures given below and write **N** for natural things and **M** for man-made things.

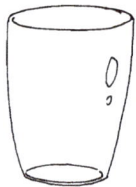

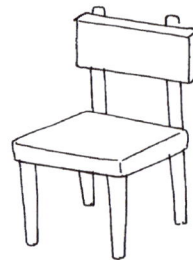

B. Look at the pictures give below and circle all the natural things which are non-living.

C. Complete the concept map given below.

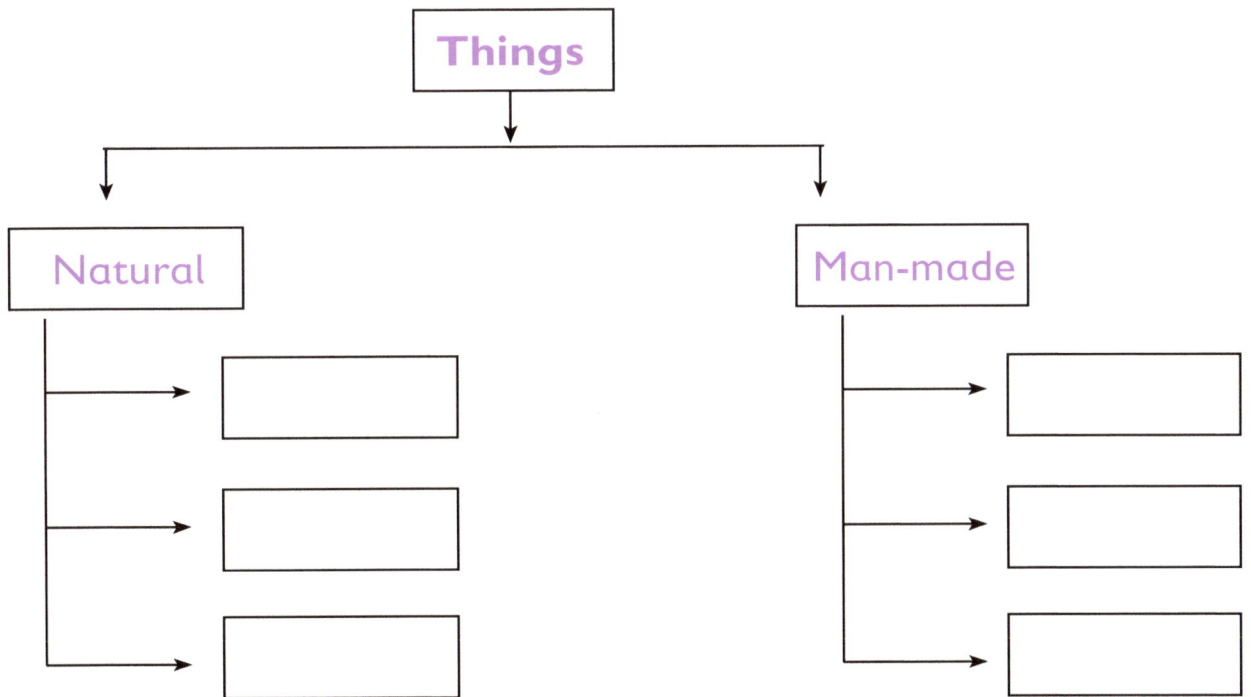

```
                        Things
                          │
        ┌─────────────────┼─────────────────┐
        ▼                                    ▼
     Natural                            Man-made
        │                                    │
        ├──────▶  [        ]                 ├──────▶  [        ]
        │                                    │
        ├──────▶  [        ]                 ├──────▶  [        ]
        │                                    │
        └──────▶  [        ]                 └──────▶  [        ]
```

Plants

Plants are living things which grow in soil. There are several plants around us. Some are big, some are small. They have different parts such as roots, leaves, stem, flowers and fruits.

A. Can you label the parts of the plant given below using the help box?

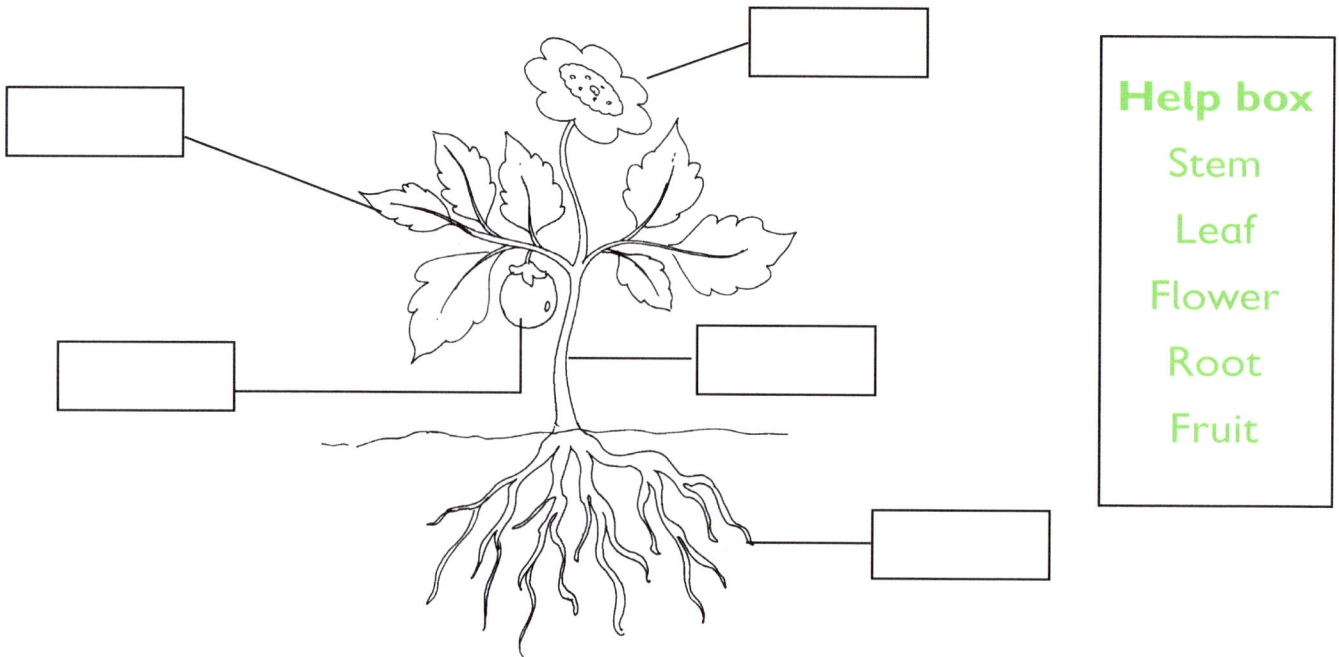

Help box

Stem

Leaf

Flower

Root

Fruit

B. Name three plants which you can find in your surroundings.

C. Fill in the blanks with the correct words.

trees	seeds	sun	leaves	soil	Roots

1. Big plants are called _____ .

2. _____ absorb water for the plants.

3. New plants grow from _____ .

4. Plants grow in the _____ .

5. Plants get energy from the _____.

6. Food for the plant is prepared in the _____ .

D. Circle the things which a plant needs to grow.

E. Give two examples for each of the following using the words given in the help box.

	Example 1	Example 2
Trees		
Climbers		
Herbs		
Shrubs		
Creepers		

Help box
Grapes
Cotton
Apple
Pumpkin
Rose
Mint
Banana
Spinach
Peas
Watermelon

11

F. Name two plants each which:

have thorns
- ....
- ....

grow in water
- ....
- ....

have fruits
- ....
- ....

have flowers
- ....
- ....

Things We Get From Plants

Plants give us many things including most of our food. They also provide us with flowers, wood and many other things.

A. Look at the pictures given below and circle the things we get from plants.

We eat different parts of plants as food; such as seeds, leaves, fruits and stem. For example, broccoli is the flower of the broccoli plant.

B. Name the plants from which we get the given parts as food using the help box given below.

Leaves	Seeds	Stem	Root

spinach	corn	sugarcane	potato	turnip	mint
radish	gram	celery	cabbage	peas	carrot

C. Draw any six things that we get from plants.

D. Complete the concept map given below.

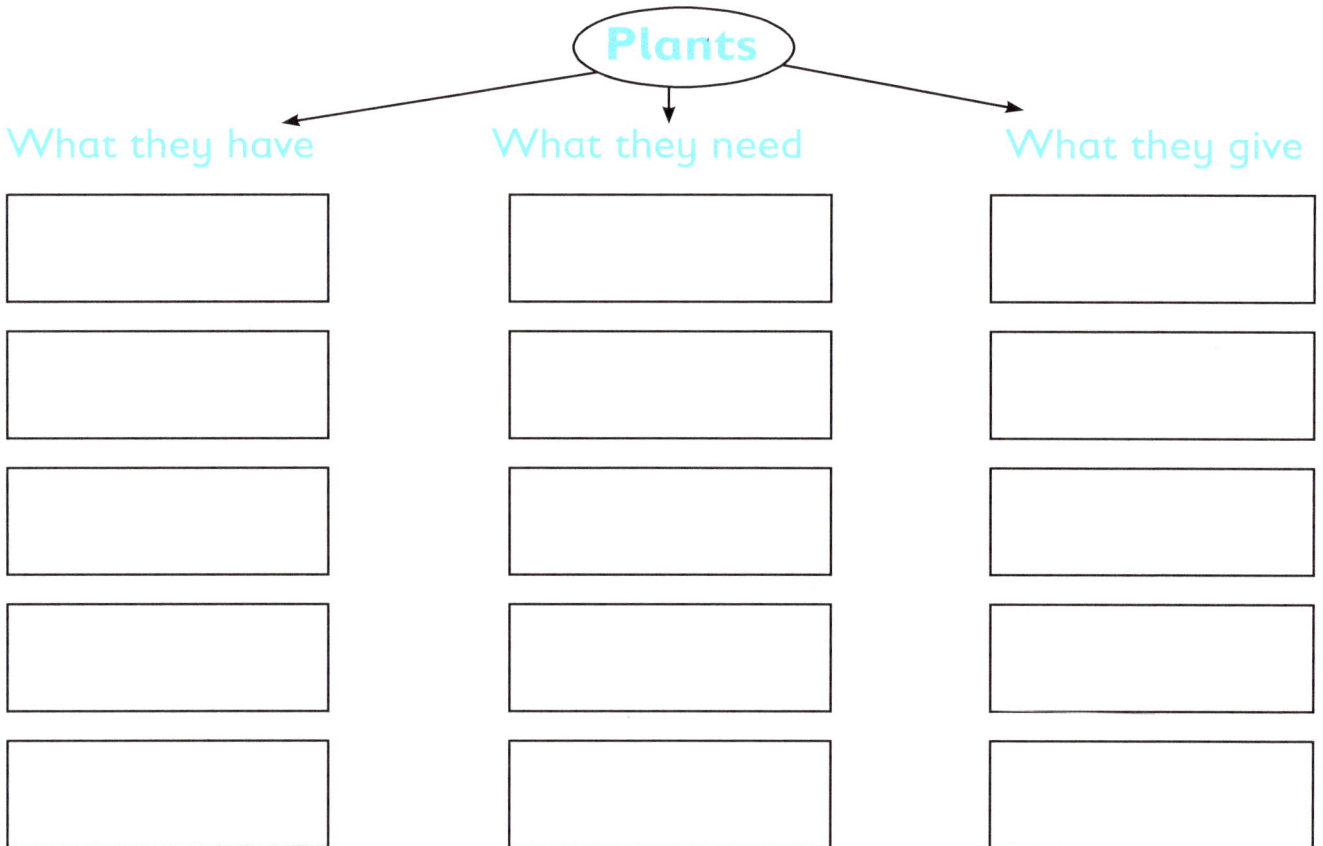

Plants

What they have   What they need   What they give

Animals

There are different kinds of animals in the world. Some animals can fly, some can swim while some can walk and climb.

Animals live in different habitats. Animals like dogs, lions and bears live on land while fishes, octopuses and whales live in water. Some animals can live both on land and in water such as frogs, crabs and crocodiles.

A. Match the following animals to their natural habitat.

Coop

Forest

Tree

Pond

Burrow

Ocean

15

B. Name two animals for each of the groups given below.

(1)	Which can fly		
(2)	Which can climb a tree		
(3)	Which can walk on ground		
(4)	Which can swim		
(5)	Which can walk and swim		

C. Fill in the blanks using words from the help box given below.

ocean	den	insect	kennel	birds	tree	cave

1. A dog lives in a _____.

2. A lion lives in a _____.

3. Pengiuns, sparrows and ducks are _____.

4. Sharks live in the _____.

5. A housefly is an _____.

6. A parrot lives on a _____.

7   A bear lives in a _____.

Animals and Their Food

All animals need food to survive. Different animals eat different kinds of food. They move from one place to another in search of food.

Small animals such as hens and squirrel eat seeds and grains. Animals such as lizard, frog and some birds eat insects and worms. Domestic animals such as cow, horse and rabbit eat plants. Wild animals such as lion and tiger eat the flesh of other animals.

A. Can you identify each animal given below and write their names in the boxes?

....	....	....	....
....	....	....	....

Animals use different parts of their body to find and eat their food. They use their claws, beak, wings, teeth and stings to catch, hold and eat food.

B. Can you write the body parts the animals given below use to eat food?

1. Frog ....

2. Bird ....

3. Squirrel ....

4. Elephant ....

5. Crocodile ....

6. Lizard ....

C. Complete the concept map given below with the correct words.

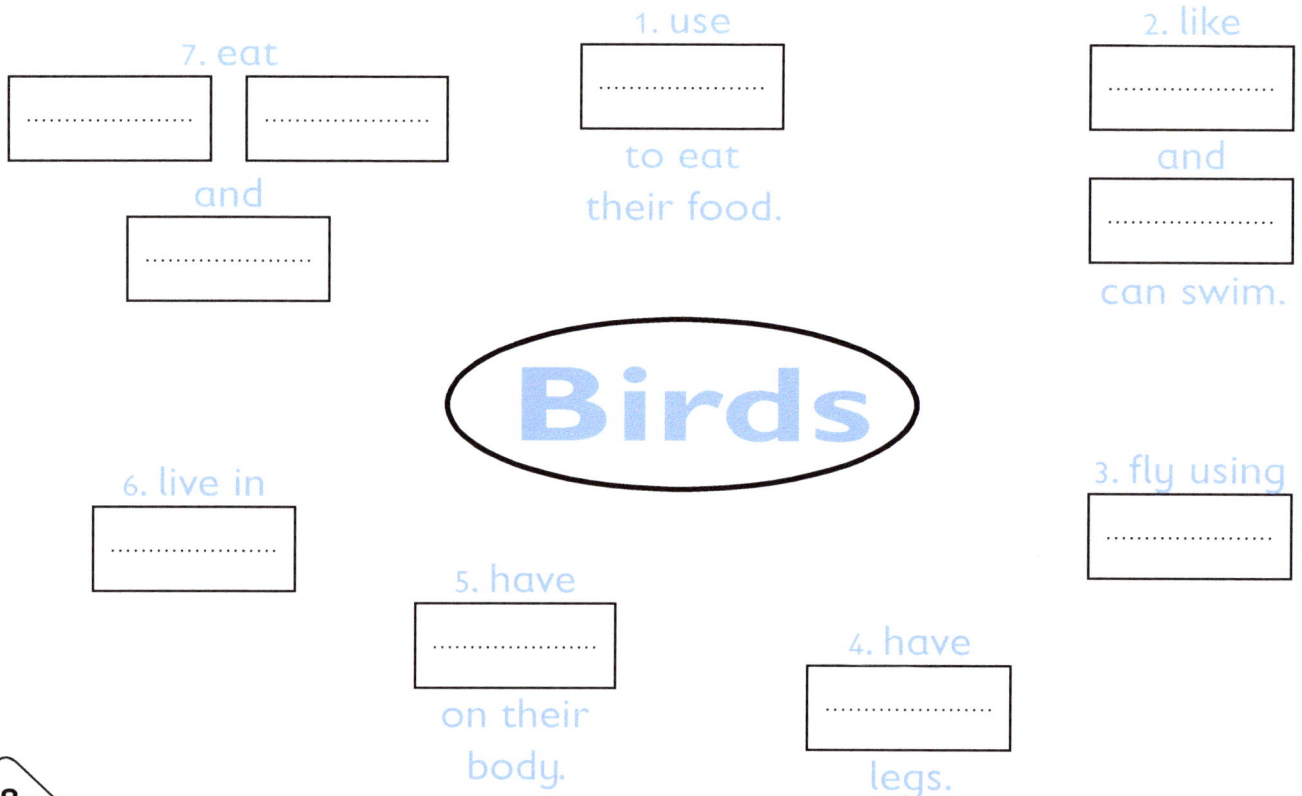

7. eat
....

and
....

1. use
....
to eat
their food.

2. like
....
and
....
can swim.

Birds

6. live in
....

5. have
....
on their
body.

4. have
....
legs.

3. fly using
....

The Human Body

Our body is made up of many parts that help us in different ways. These different body parts help us to walk, run, play, write and eat.

A. Can you find and match the body parts mentioned in the image given below?

Finger		Eye
Nose		Hair
Arm		Knee
Head		Ear
Chest		Neck
Mouth		Leg
Foot		Stomach
Eyebrows		Toes

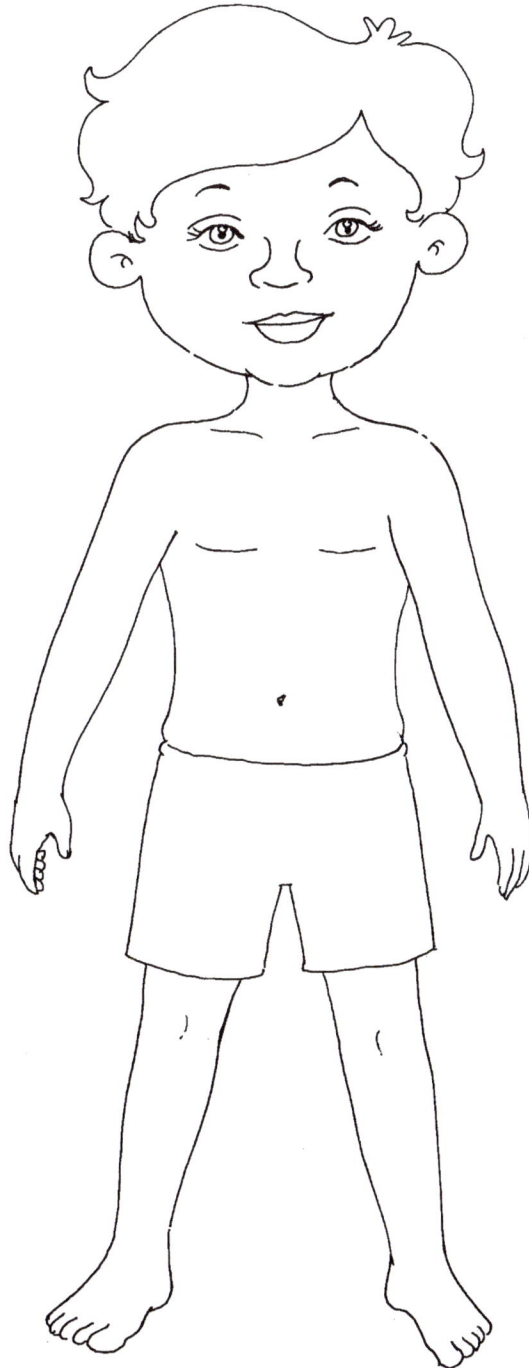

B. Name any two activities which you can perform using the given parts of your body.

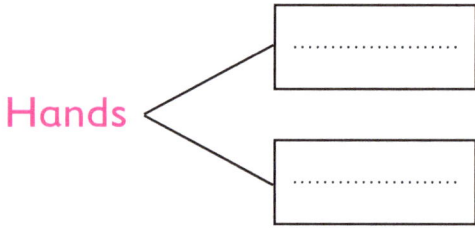

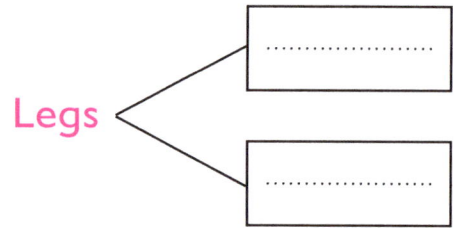

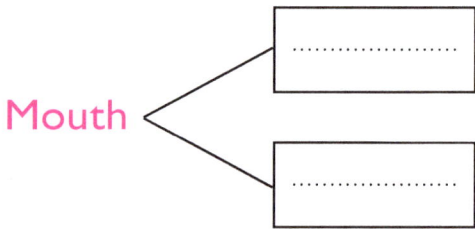

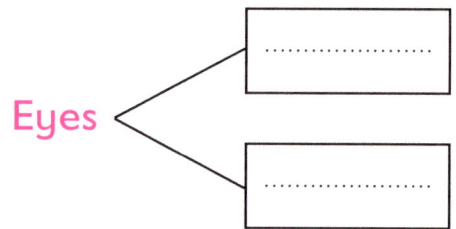

Hands ⟨
[_____]
[_____]

Legs ⟨
[_____]
[_____]

Mouth ⟨
[_____]
[_____]

Eyes ⟨
[_____]
[_____]

C. Name the sense organs you use for the following tasks.

1. Read a story _____

2. Listen to a song _____

3. Smell a perfume _____

4. Taste a lemon _____

5. Touch a leaf _____

D. Name two things that you can do without using your hands and legs.

[_____]   [_____]

E. Look at the pictures given below and circle the objects you can identify by smelling.

F. Fill in the blanks with the words from the help box.

| neck | hands | skin | tongue | hear | legs |

1. Our _____ help us to write.

2. We can feel soft and hard surfaces with our _____.

3. Our _____ helps us to move our head.

4. The _____ helps us to taste.

5. We use our _____ to play football.

6. Our ears help us to _____.

Food

All living things need food to survive. Food gives us energy and helps us to grow. We get food from plants and animals. We must eat fresh, clean and healthy food, and include different items of food in our diet to stay fit and healthy.

A. Write P for the food items you get from plants and A for the items you get from animals below.

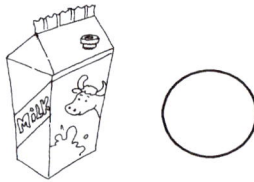

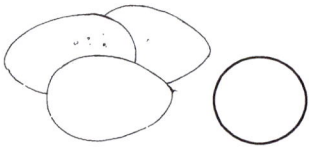

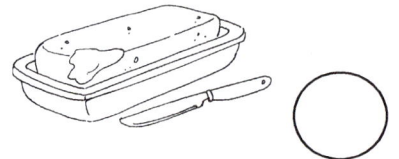

B. Fill in the blanks with the correct option.

1. We get _____ from plants. (milk/potatoes)

2. _____ fruits help us to stay fit. (Fresh/ Dirty)

3. We get eggs from _____ . (hen/goat)

4. _____ makes our bones and teeth strong. (Water/Milk)

5. We make _____ from milk. (curd/mango)

6. Food gives us _____. (honey/energy)

7. We must eat when we are hungry, but not _____. (overeat/eat)

8. _____ things need food to grow. (Living/Non-living)

C. Give two examples for each of the following.

1. Food from animals.

2. Food from plants.

3. Food made from milk.

4. Food you like to eat.

5. Unhealthy food.

D. Complete the concept map given below.

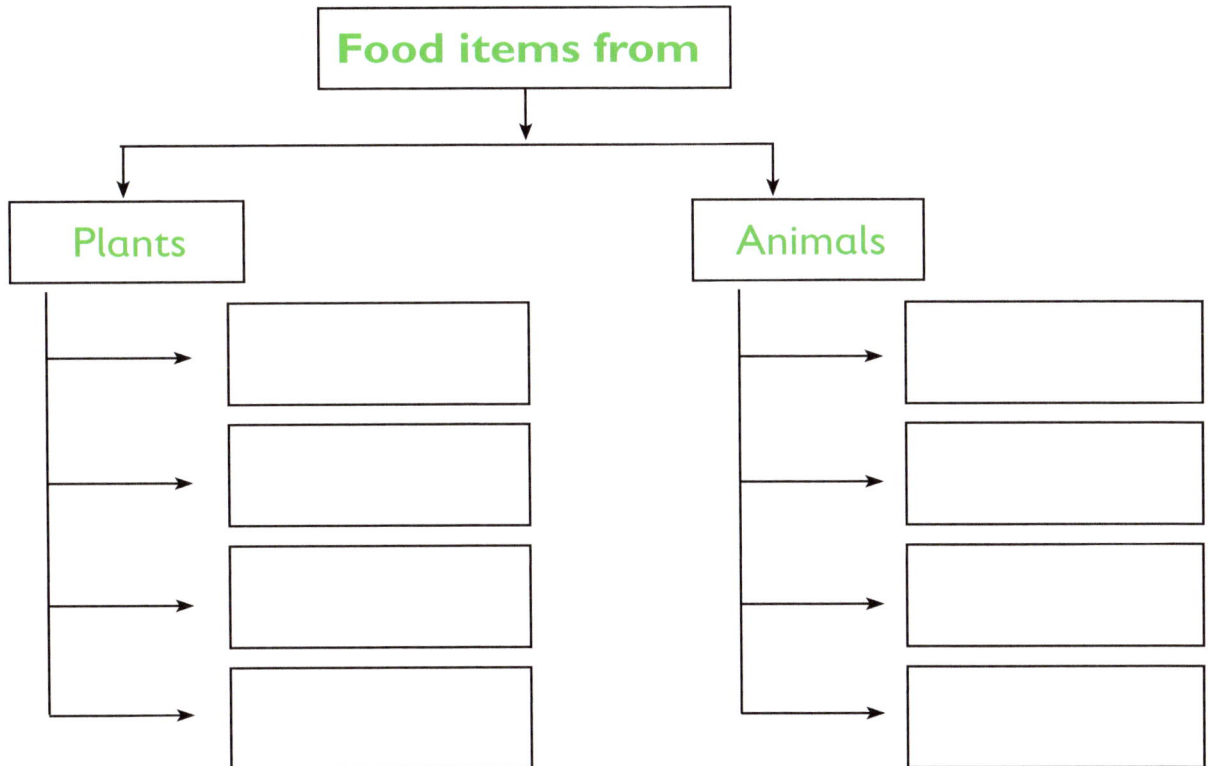

Food items from

Plants

Animals

House

We all live in a house. It protects us from bad weather, wild animals and criminals. Different rooms in our houses are meant for different purposes. We must keep our house clean.

A. Look at the picture of a house below and label the rooms using the help box.

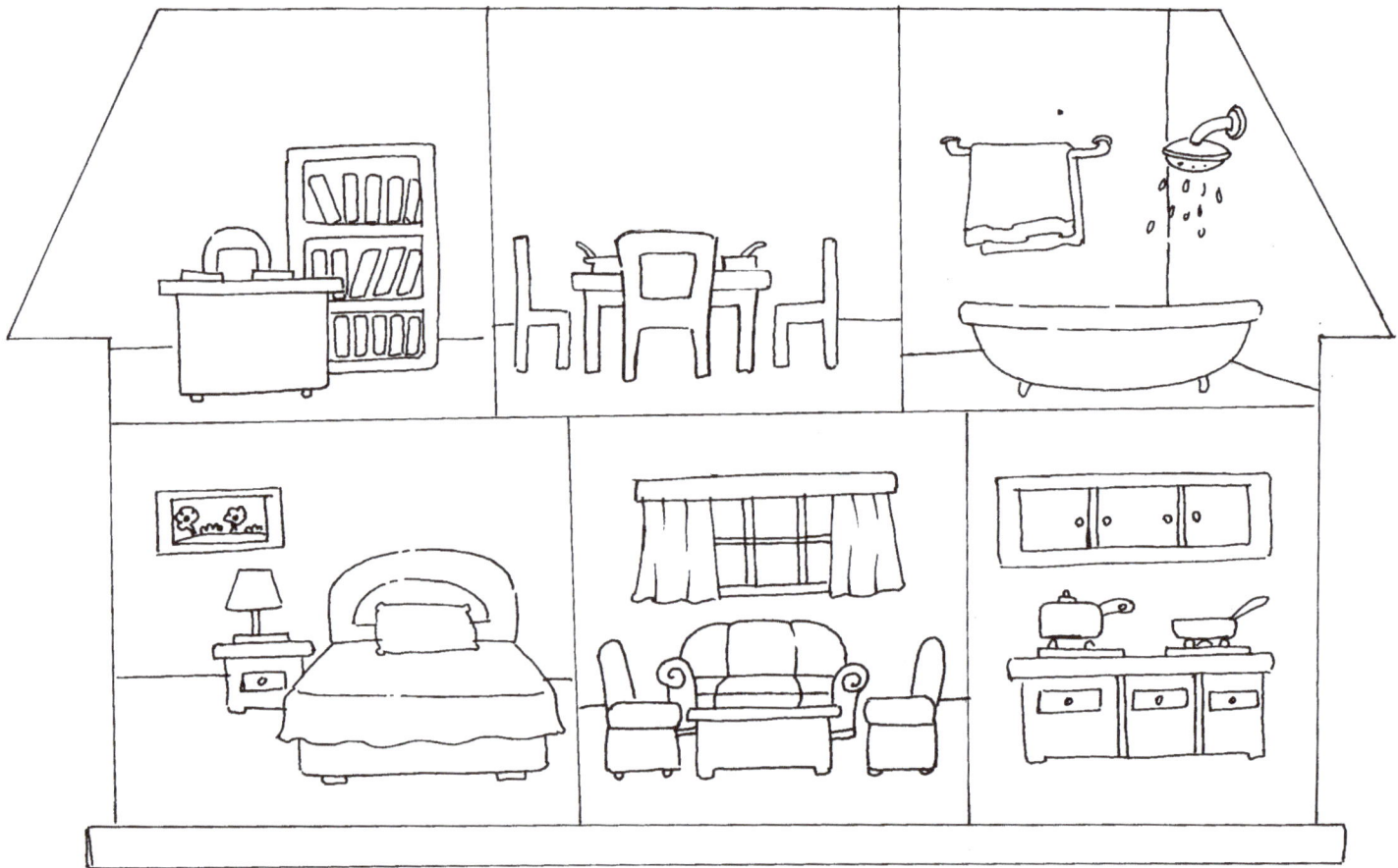

Help Box

Living room	Dining room
Kitchen	Study room
Bathroom	Bedroom

B. Fill in the blanks with the correct words.

sleep	living room	bath	study	kitchen

1. We take a _____ in the bathroom.

2. We prepare food in the _____.

3. We read in the _____ room.

4. We _____ in our bedroom.

5. We attend guests in the _____.

C. Go around your house and find where these objects are kept and write it down.

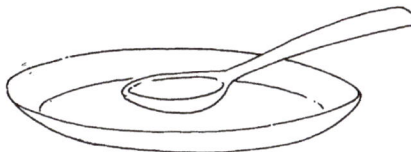

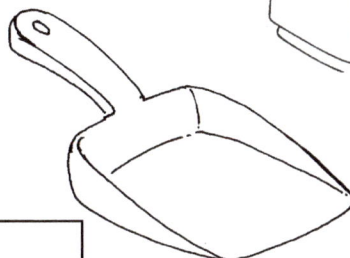

....

....

....

....

....

D. **Read the statement given below and write T for true statements and F for false ones.**

1. Our house protects us from bad weather and wild animals. ☐

2. Our house protects us from flowers and trees. ☐

3. We sleep in our bathroom. ☐

4. We eat our food in the dining room. ☐

5. We must keep our house clean and airy. ☐

E. **Look at the pictures given below. Circle the things from which our house protects us.**

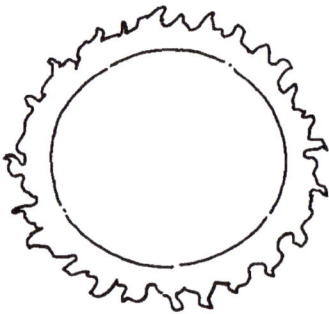

Clothes

We need clothes to protect our body from cold, heat, wind and rain. They also make us look beautiful. We wear outfits according to the weather and occassion. We have different outfits to wear for different parts of our body.

A. Can you match the clothes to the body parts that they are made for?

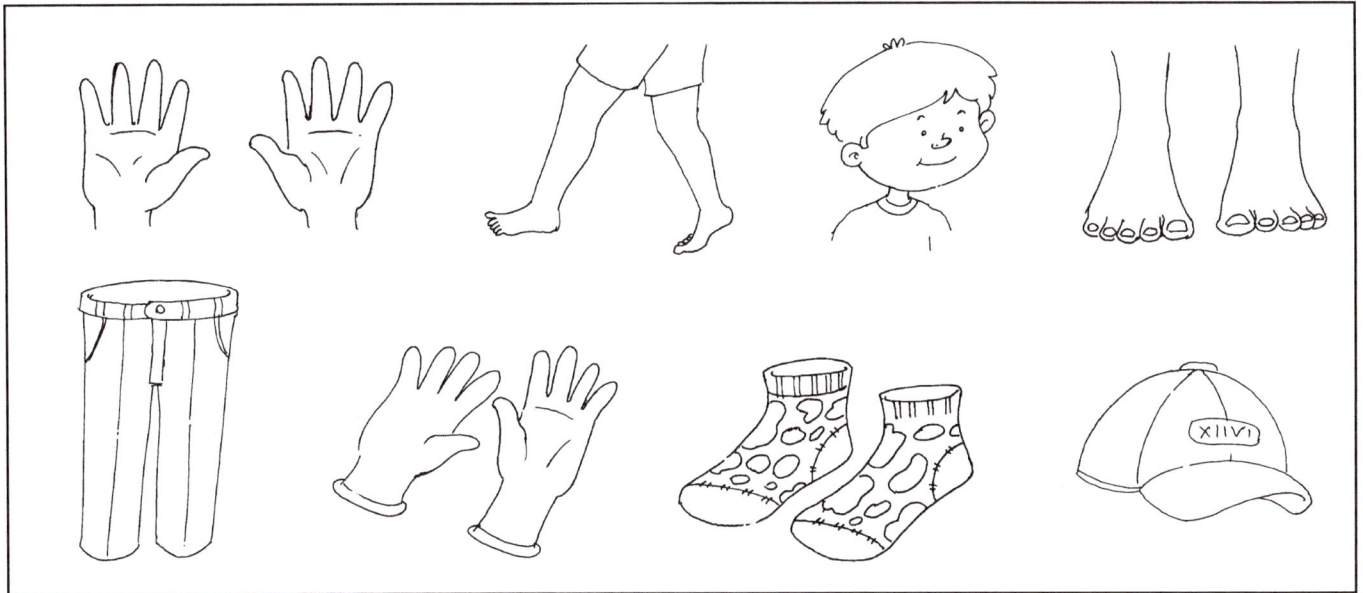

B. Write C for the clothes which you would wear on a cold day and H for the clothes which you would wear on a hot day.

C.   Fill in the blanks with the correct words.

raincoat   cotton   beautiful   woollen   heat

1. We wear _____ clothes on a hot day.

2. We wear _____ clothes on a cold day.

3. We wear a _____ on a raing day.

4. Clothes protect us from _____, wind and rain.

5. Clothes make us look _____.

D.   Can you fill in the blanks looking at the given picture clues?

D__ES__

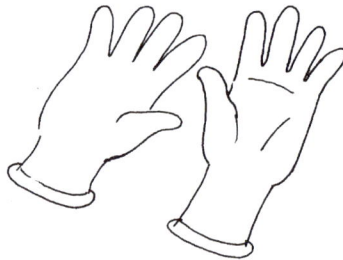

G__ __V__S

SH__R__

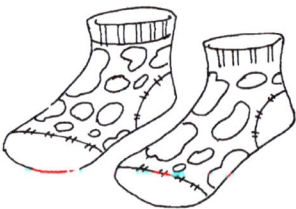

S__ __KS

__OO__S

C__A__

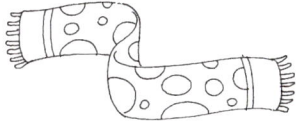

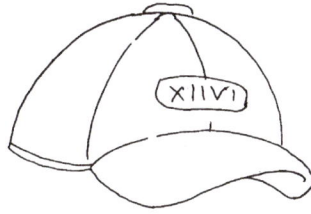

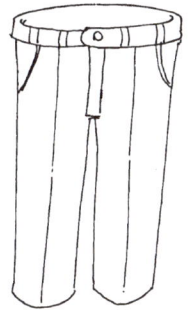

| S__ __ RF | C__ P | P__NTS |

E. Complete the concept map given below.

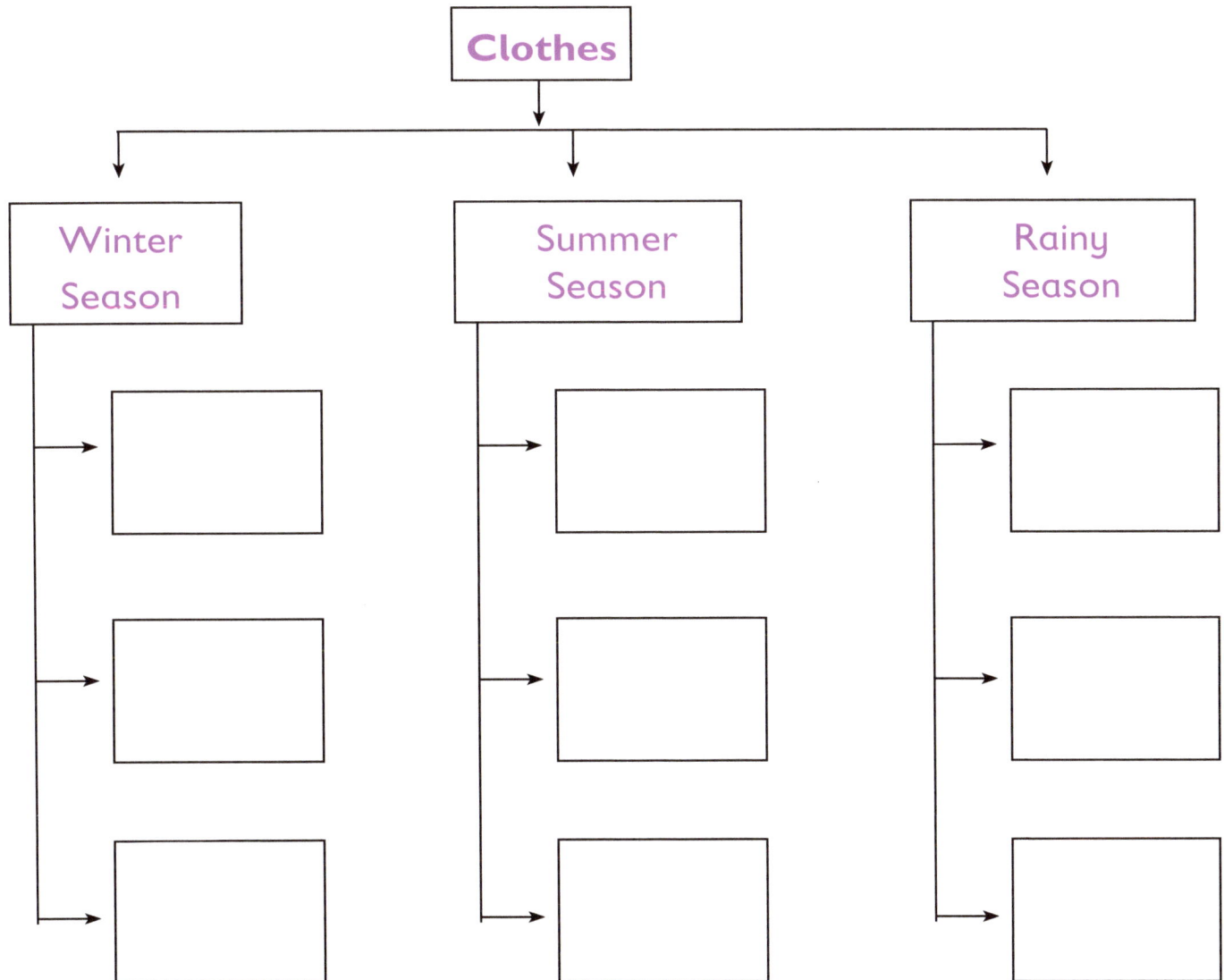

Clean and Healthy

We must keep our body and surroundings clean to stay healthy. A balanced diet, exercise and a good sleep help us to remain healthy and fit. The habit of being and keeping the surroundings clean is called cleanliness.

A. Look at the pictures given below and match the activities in cloumn A to the correct pictures in column B.

Column A	Column B
• Brush twice a day	
• Sleep eight hours daily	
• Trim nails	
• Exercise daily	
• Wear clean clothes	
• Bathe daily	

B. Write T for true statements and F for false ones.

1. Biting nails is a good habit. ☐

2. Throwing waste in the dustbin keeps our surroundings clean. ☐

3. We should brush our teeth once in two days. ☐

4. We should wash our hands only after eating food. ☐

5. Sleeping for eight hours every night keeps us fit and healthy. ☐

6. We should not wash our hair. ☐

C. Name three things that you use to keep yourself clean.

D. Name three activities that you practice to keep yourself healthy.

E. Complete the crossword puzzle with the help of the clues given below.

```
                    1
                    B
        2
        T  R        M

             3
             S  L     E  P
     4
     W  A  S
```

1. _____ your teeth.

2. _____ your nails.

3. _____ for eight hours.

4. _____ your hands with soap.

Safety for All

Safety is being careful and protecting oneself from danger. We must always be cautious and follow all the safety rules. Safety rules should be followed at home, in school and all other places such as the park, the library, the market etc. One should inform a teacher or an adult if they feel unsafe.

A. Look at the pictures given below and cross out the ones that show unsafe actions.

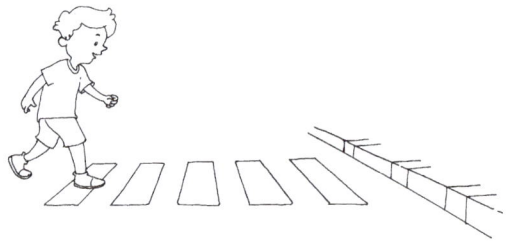

B. Name four road signs which you can see on the roads.

C. Name four objects which are used for the safety of people.

D. Fill in the blanks with the correct words from the help box.

run	burn	red	queue	footpath

1. Playing with fire can _____ your hand.

2. Always walk on the _____.

3. Make a _____ while getting on a bus.

4. Cross the road when the traffic light is _____.

5 Do not _____ in the school corridors.

E. Name two things which you should not play with in order to be safe.

F. Name two places where you should not go alone in order to stay safe.

G. Colour the traffic light below and fill in the blanks with the correct answers.

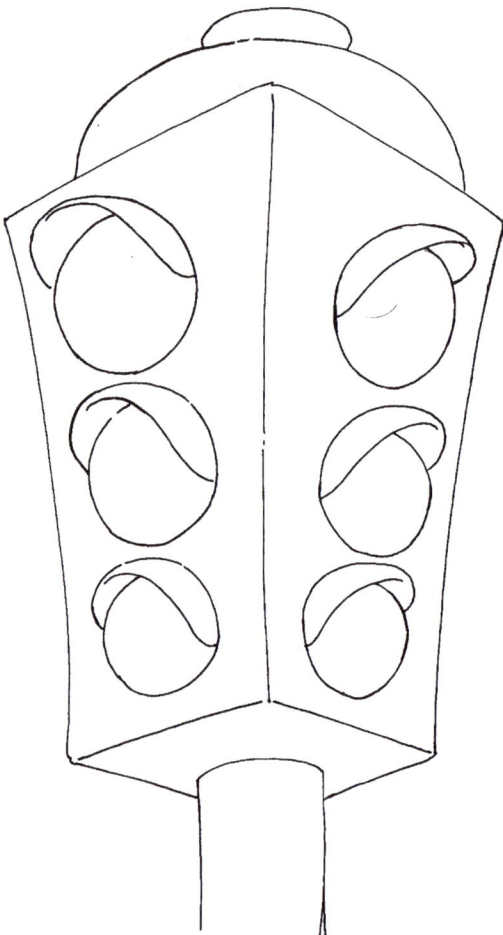

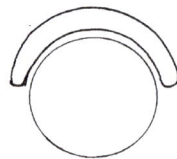

Red light means

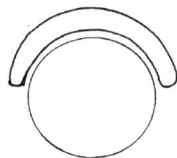

Amber light means

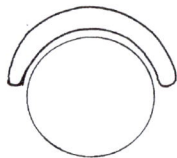

Green light means

Air

Air is a mixture of gases around us. We cannot see air, but we can feel it. It has no colour or smell, but it has mass and weight. Moving air is called wind. All living things need air to breathe. It can also move things like a kite, a balloon or even a sailboat.

A. Look at the pictures given below and cross out the things which do not need air to move.

B. Give two examples for each of the following.

1. Things that can be filled with air.

2. Things that need air to live.

3. Things that can be moved by wind.

[   ]   [   ]

C. State whether the given statements are True (T) or False (F).

1. We cannot light a fire without air. [   ]

2. We can fill water in a football in the absence of air. [   ]

3. Air makes the train move faster. [   ]

4. Air occupies space and has weight. [   ]

5. Moving air is used to generate electricity. [   ]

D. Draw two means of transport which require air in order to move.

| | |
| | |

Water

Living things need water to live. We get water from different sources such as rivers, rain, wells and lakes. We use water in our daily routine for cleaning, cooking, drinking and other purposes. We must use clean water and never waste it. Throwing waste into water sources makes the water unfit for use.

A. Look at the pictures of different sources of water given below and use the picture clues to complete their names.

W__L__

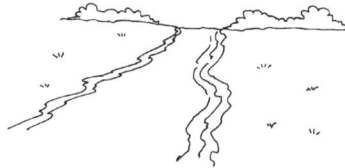

R__ __ER

L__ __E

WA __ E __FA__ __

R__I__

HA__ D PU__P

B. Match the following:

Column A	Column B
• River water is stored in	lakes
• At home, water is stored in	well
• Clean water is used for	dams
• Rain water fills up the	drinking
• An underground water source	tanks

C. Tick (✔) the activities in which water is not wasted.

D. Fill in the blanks with the correct option.

1. A _____ is built to hold back water. (dam/tap)

2. We should _____ water. (waste/save)

3. Drinking _____ water can make us ill. (clean/dirty)

4. Water is also used to put out a _____. (fire/plant)

5. Water is delivered to our homes through _____. (ocean/pipes)

E. Complete the concept map given below.

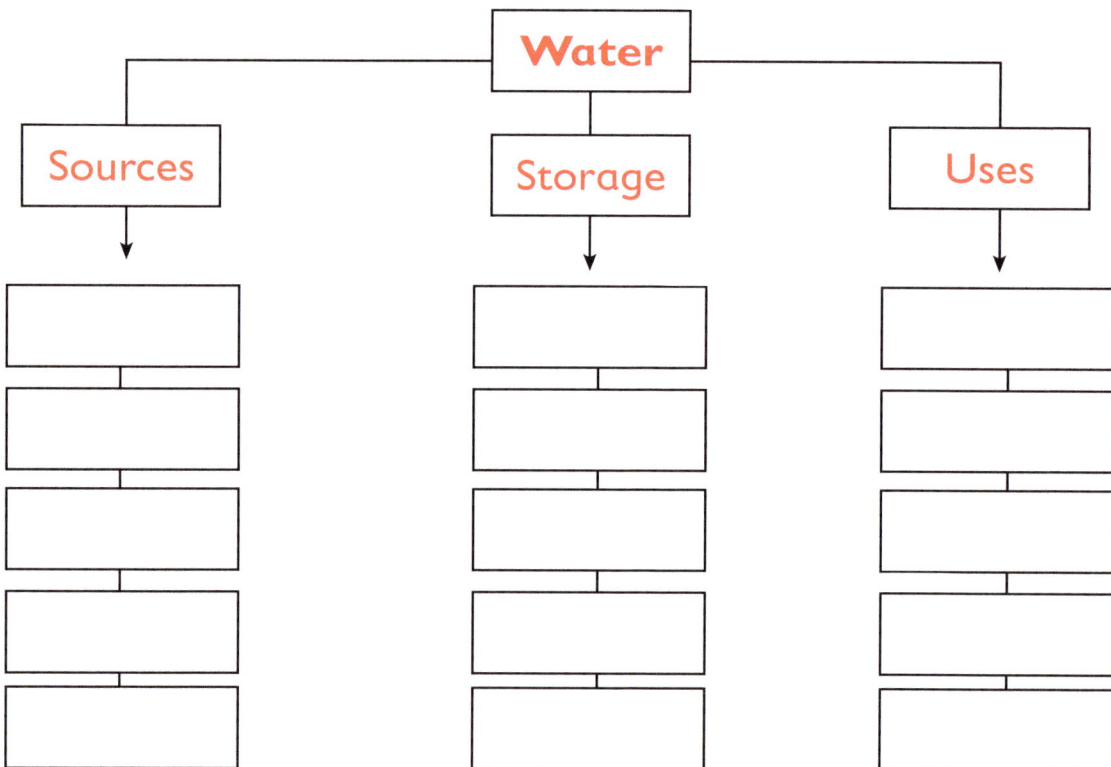

Water

Sources

Storage

Uses

The Sun, Moon and Stars

The sun is a big, yellow ball of fire. It is very hot and shines brightly during the day. It gives heat and light to all living things. The moon looks like a big white ball and can be seen clearly at night. The changing shapes of the moon are called phases of the moon.

Stars are the tiny dots which shine brightly at night. They make patterns in the sky. The sun is also a star. It appears bigger in size because it is nearer to us than the other stars.

A. Look at the pictures given below. Match the pictures to their names.

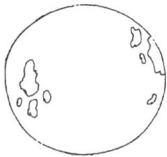   Crescent Moon

   Star

   Full Moon

   Earth

   Sun

   Half Moon

B. Write one word for the following:

1. It gives us heat and light. _____

2. It twinkles in the sky. _____

3. It changes its shape every day. _____

4. The sun rises in this direction. _____

5. The sun sets in this direction. _____

C. Read the statements given below and write T for the statements which stand true and F for the false statements.

1. The Earth revolves around the moon. ☐

2. The sun is a star. ☐

3. The moon changes its shape every day. ☐

4. The sun gives us light and heat. ☐

5. Stars are very close to the Earth. ☐

6. The moon gets light from the Earth. ☐

D. Draw two things which you see in the day sky.

Weather & Seasons

The changes in the atmosphere from day to day is called weather. The weather can be hot, cold, dry, rainy or windy.

The different types of weathers are given below. Observe the difference in clothes and atmosphere in different weathers depending on which, we have four seasons. They are summer, monsoon, autumn and winter.

Summer

Winter

Monsoon

Autumn

A. Match the following:

Column A	Column B
Summer	It is neither too hot nor too cold.
Monsoon	It is very hot.
Autumn	It is very cold.
Winter	It rains for many days.

B. Fill in the blanks with the correct words.

| rains | Wind | warm | weather | cool |

1. Cotton clothes keep our body _____ in summers.

2. Woollen clothes keep our body _____ in winters.

3. It _____ for many days during the monsoon season.

4. _____ can blow the leaves away.

5. The _____ changes from day to day.

C. Write one word for the following:

1. The clothes worn on cold days. _____

2. The season when it rains heavily. _____

3. The clothes worn on hot days are made of this. _____

4. The season when it is very cold. _____

5. The season when it is neither too hot nor too cold. _____

D. The pictures given below are of objects that we see on a rainy day. Use the picture clues to complete their names.

RA __ __ B __ W

U __ __ __ REL __ A

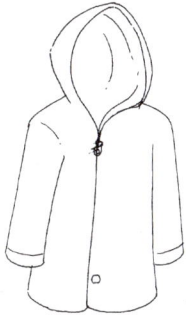

RAI __ C ___ T

G ___ ___ B __ OTS

C ___ ___ U __

F __ O __

E. Complete the concept map given below by writing the correct name of the seasons.

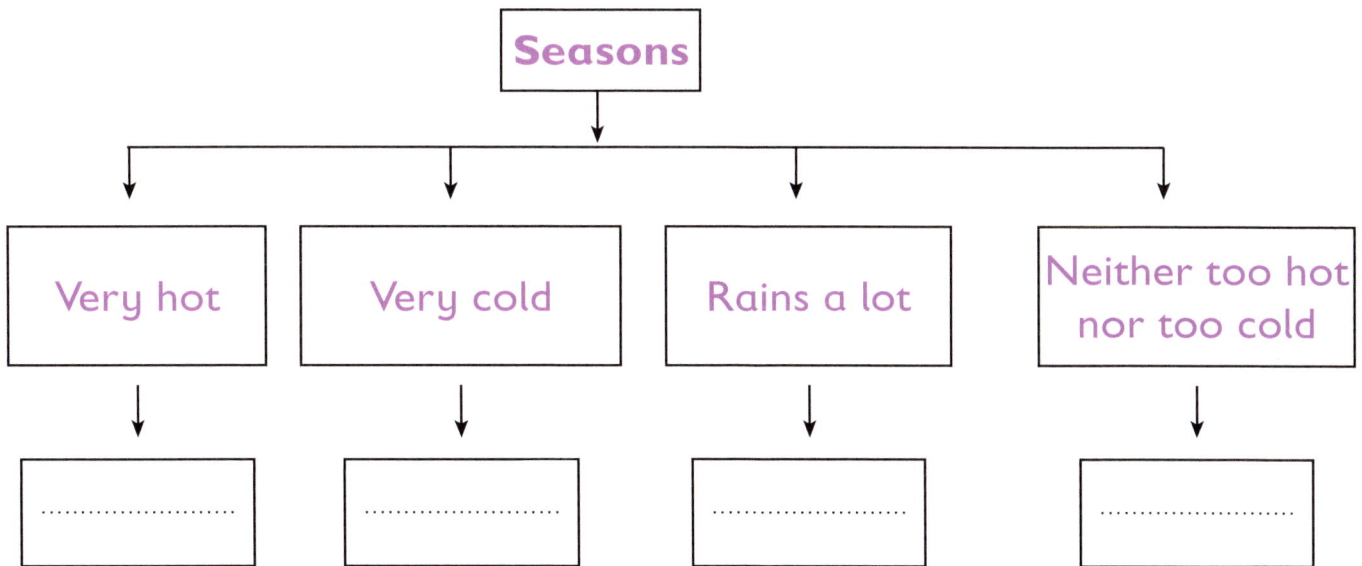

Test Yourself

A. Look at the pictures given below and name the things that you need to survive and grow.

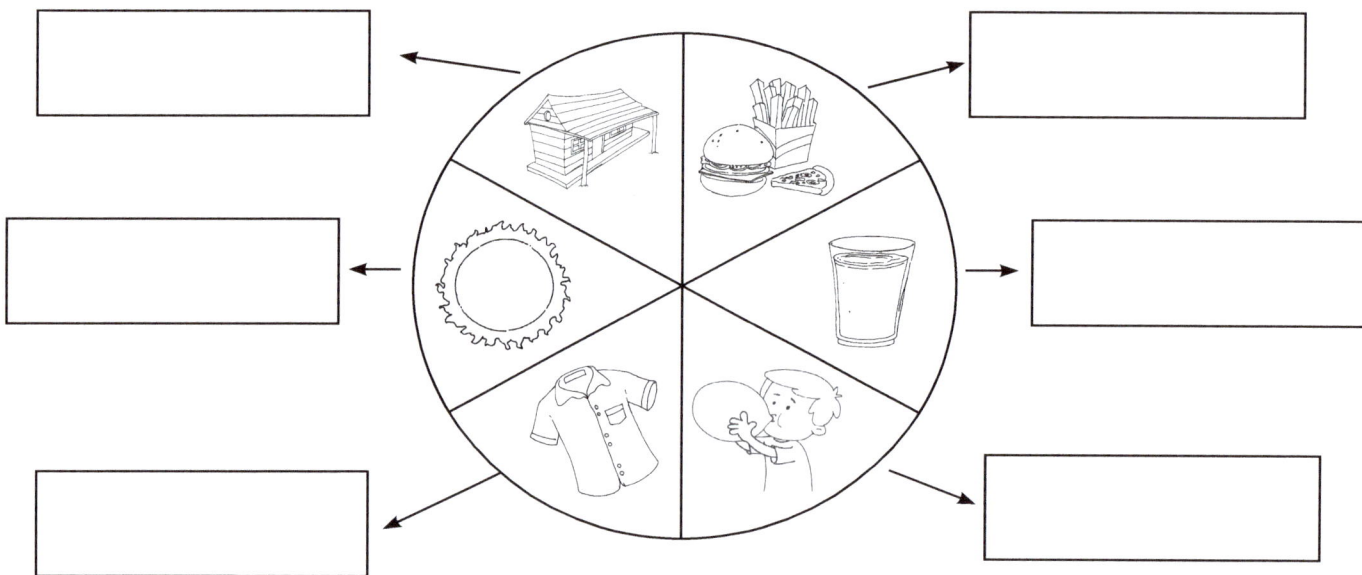

B. Read the statements given below and write T for true statements and F for false ones.

1. We can see the stars when it's raining.

2. The moon changes its shape every day.

3. It gets dark after sunrise.

4. Moving air is called wind.

5. The weather is very hot in the summer season.

C. Look at the pictures given below and circle the ones that need air.

D. Fill in the blanks with the correct words.

wild animals	kitchen	sun	knife	moon

1. We can see the _____ in the sky only during the day.

2. The shape of the _____ changes every day.

3. A house protects us from harsh weather and _____.

4. It is unsafe to play with a _____.

5. We should not play in the _____.

E. Look at the pictures given below and name the objects.

E. Look at the pictures given below and name the objects.

Answers

Our Surroundings

A. Bicycle, car, house, tree, animal, road
B. Bird, shop, tree, bicycle
C. Drain pipe, Garbage
D. Car, bicycle, trees, animals, street light, stones
E. Plants, road signs, stones, bus, car
F. 1. clean   2. Dirty   3. dustbin
     4. Plants   5. trees

Living and Non-living Things

A. Living things: boy, dog, plants, bird
     Non-living things: shoes, kite
B. Plants, Boy, Girl, Dog, Cat, etc.
C. Car, Table, Book, pencil, etc.
D. Air, Water, Soil
E. 1. breathe   2. water   3. Non-living
     4. soil   5. food

Natural and Man-made Things

A. Natural things: flower, milk, bird, cloud
     Man-made things: book, glass, toy, chair
B. Water in river, soil in pot
C. Natural: mountains, sky, river, soil, flowers, etc.
     Man-made: mobiles, phones, laptops, beds, forts, etc.

Plants

B. Aloe Vera, Tulsi, Neem, Rose, etc.
C. 1. trees   2. Roots   3. seeds
     4. soil   5. sun   6. leaves
D. Soil, Sun, Water
E. Trees: Apple, Banana
     Climbers: Grapes, Peas
     Herbs: Mint, Spinach
     Shrubs: Rose, Cotton
     Creeper: Pumpkin, Watermelon
F. Plants with thorns: Rose, Cactus
     Plants with fruits: Banana, Mango
     Plants with flowers: Rose, Dahlia
     Plants that grow in water: Lotus, Duckweed

Things We Get From Plants

A. Apple, cotton shirt, perfume, wooden pencil, jute rope
B. Leaves: spinach, cabbage, mint
     Seeds: corn, peas, gram
     Stem: sugarcane, potato, celery
     Root: radish, carrot, turnip
D. What plants have: Roots, Stem, Leaves, Flowers, Fruits
     What they need: Air, Water, Sunlight, Soil, Minerals
     What they give: Food, Flowers, Fibre, Wood, Rubber

Animals

B. 1. Crow, Bee, Butterfly
     2. Monkey, Cat, Ant
     3. Elephant, Tiger, Dog, Horse
     4. Fish, Shark, Octopus
     5. Duck, Tortoise, Penguin
C. 1. kennel   2. den   3. birds
     4. ocean   5. insect   6. tree
     7. cave

Animals and Their Food

A. 1. Rabbit   2. Goat   3. Frog
     4. Lizard   5. Hen   6. Squirrel
     7. Lion   8. Crocodile
B. 1. Tongue   2. Beak   3. Teeth
     4. Trunk   5. Snout, Teeth   6. Tongue
C. Birds eat seeds, worms and insects.
     Birds live in nests.
     Birds that can swim: Penguin, Duck
     Birds have two legs.
     Birds have feathers on their body.
     Birds fly using their wings.
     Birds use their beaks to eat food.

The Human Body

B. Hands: write, hold, pull and push
     Legs: walk, run and kick
     Mouth: speak, eat and whistle
     Eyes: see, stare and wink
C. 1. Eyes and Mouth   2. Ears
     3. Nose   4. Tongue
     5. Fingers (skin)
D. Watching movie, Sleeping, Speaking, Listening etc.
E. Rose, Coffee or Tea, Garbage, Cookies
F. 1. hand   2. skin   3. neck
     4. tongue   5. legs   6. hear

Food

A. Food items from plants: fruits, pulses, rice, vegetables
     Food items from animals: milk, eggs, meat, butter
B. 1. potatoes   2. Fresh   3. hen
     4. Milk   5. curd   6. energy
     7. overeat   8. Living
C. 1. Milk, Egg   2. Apple, Potato
     3. Butter, Curd   4. Answers may vary
     5. Burger, Packed food
D. Food items from plants: coffee, wheat, sugar, tea
     Food items from animals: milk, oil, meat, egg

House

B. 1. Bath   2. kitchen   3. study
     4. sleep   5. living room
D. 1. T   2. F   3. F
     4. T   5. T
E. Rain, Cold, Wild Animals, Burglar

Clothes

B. 1. C   2. C   3. H
     4. H   5. C   6. H
C. 1. cotton   2. woollen   3. raincoat
     4. heat   5. beautiful
D. 1. Dress   2. Gloves   3. Shirt
     4. Socks   5. Boots   6. Coat
     7. Scarf   8. Cap   9. Pants
E. Winter season: Sweater, Scarf, Coat
     Summer season: Shorts, Skirt, T-shirt
     Rainy season: Raincoat, Gumboots, Cap

Clean and Healthy

B. 1. F   2. T   3. F
4. F   5. T   6. F
C. Soap, Towel, Shampoo, Tooth paste
D. Exercise, Rest, Drinking Water, Eating healthy food
E. 1. Brush   2. Trim
3. Sleep   4. Wash

Safety for All

B. Traffic light, Stop, No Parking, Crossover bridge
C. Zebra crossing, Footpath, Seat belt, Helmet
D. 1. burn   2. footpath
3. queue   4. red
5. run
E. Fire, Knife, Scissor
F. Zoo, Swimming pool
G. Red light means stop.
Amber light means get ready.
Green light means go.

Air

B. 1. Balloon, Swimming Tube
2. Plants, Animals, Humans
3. Kite, Cloth, Fallen leaves, Paper
C. 1. T   2. F
3. F   4. T
5. T

Water

A. 1. Well   2. River   3. Lake
4. Waterfall   5. Rain   6. Hand pump
C. 1. and 3.
D. 1. dam   2. save   3. dirty
4. fire   5. pipes
E. Sources of water:
Rain, River, Lake, Tube well, Well, Pond, etc.
Storage of water:
Tanks, Dams, Cans, Bottles, Underground storage,
Barrels, etc.
Uses of water:
Drinking, Cooking, Cleaning, Bathing, Watering
plants, etc.

The Sun, Moon and Stars

B. 1. Sun   2. Star   3. Moon
4. East   5. West
C. 1. F   2. T   3. T
4. T   5. F   6. F

Weather and Seasons

B. 1. cool   2. warm
3. rains   4. Wind
5. weather
C. 1. Woollen   2. Monsoon
3. Cotton   4. Winter
5. Autumn
D. 1. Rainbow   2. Umbrella
3. Raincoat   4. Gumboots
5. Cloud   6. Frog
E. Very hot: Summer
Very Cold: Winter
Rains a lot: Monsoon
Neither too hot nor too cold: Autumn

Test Yourself

A. House, Sun, Clothes, Air, Water, Food
B. 1. F   2. T
3. F   4. T
5. T
C. Swimming Tube, Bird, Plant
D. 1. sun   2. moon
3. wild animals   4. knife
5. kitchen
E. Tap, Sun, Traffic light, Half Moon, Well, Kite, Windmill,
Clouds, Scarf

www.ingramcontent.com/pod-product-compliance
Lightning Source LLC
Chambersburg PA
CBHW060810270326
41928CB00002B/45